The Perfected Scripture of the Life Receiving Golden Seals of the Five Dippers as Spoken by Taishang Laojun

Translated by

Joshua Paynter 理文

Jack Schaefer 理玄

D1677863

CONTENTS

DISCLAIMER:

We have exercised due diligence in the translation of this scripture and take full responsibility for errors and omissions.

The pinyin Romanization of the People's Republic of China was adopted throughout this book. Proper names, titles, and formalized concepts have all been capitalized. Similar words to these titles which are conceptual have not been capitalized.

The Chinese text has been formatted and punctuated in the same way as the source text for consistency. We have chosen to format the text using traditional Chinese characters for consistency with the source text. We have added the associated pinyin to aid in making the text useful for chanting practice. Additionally, the table of contents has been formatted to make reference easy between the English and Chinese equivalent texts.

PARTING CLOUDS
DAOIST EDUCATION

ACKNOWLEDGMENTS

We would like to thank our Parting Clouds community. Without the companionship and support from this ever-growing group of people, there would be no translations of this sort. The sincerity and seriousness that this community embodies is a constant prompt for us to continue contributing translations of Daoist writings to the English speaking world.

INTRODUCTION

I was first introduced to this text by one of my teachers, Jiang Changming 蔣常明. He was utilizing this scripture in the performance of the ritual for consecrating a statue, which is called "opening light", or kaiguang 開光. This text and the talismans within were of immediate interest to me. As soon as I read it, I knew it would be of great value to others as well. This translation soon followed.

Though short in length, this scripture is a treasure trove of Daoist doctrine relating to cosmology and the genesis of human life as we revolve in the cycle of death and rebirth. From where does the human form receive its gifts of matter and animation? How does karma become manifest in our coalescing forms deep in the beginnings of each incarnation? How do we integrate essential concepts from the Chinese natural sciences into the systems of Daoist ethics and cosmology? Some of these questions are answered here in the surface of this scripture. Others are woven into deeper layers of meanings only evident after dedicated study.

Who might be interested in these questions? Who might this scripture serve? There are three main communities for whom this will be useful and interesting: Daoists, Chinese medicine practitioners, and Martial artists. It is a text of devotion, healing, empowerment, and so much more. I hope that anyone looking within these pages can find inspiration and hopefully a deeper sense of the Daoist tradition.

Jack Schaefer and I hope this text is an aid to your study and practice of Daoism. As we continue to build stronger communities among Daoists worldwide, it is our intention that all of our translations form part of the connective tissue that binds us all together as practitioners.

Josh Paynter 裴理文
Co-Abbot
Parting Clouds
Daoist Education

THE PERFECTED SCRIPTURE OF THE LIFE RECEIVING GOLDEN SEALS OF THE FIVE DIPPERS AS SPOKEN BY TAISHANG LAOJUN

The Perfected Scripture of the Life Receiving Golden Seals of the Five Dippers as Spoken by Taishang Laojun

At that Time,

Taishang Laojun, atop the realm of Great Clarity, amidst of the Great Red Heaven[1],

within the Yellow-gold Hall, convened with the Five Elder Imperial Sovereigns:

The Eastern Dipper Sovereign Who Records and Tallies.

The Southern Dipper Sovereign Who Submits the Life Records.

The Western Dipper Sovereign Who Registers the Names.

The Northern Dipper Sovereign Who Receives the Dead.

The Central Dipper Sovereign Who Leads the Inspections.

The Nine Heavens Sovereign of Life and Spirit.

The Nine Heavens Sovereign Who Imparts Life.

The Nine Heavens Sovereign Who Imparts Good Fortune.

The Nine Heavens Sovereign Who Calculates the Rolls and Tallies.

The Nine Heavens Sovereign Treasury of Wealth and Good Fortune.

The Nine Heavens Sovereign Who Dispels Calamities and Disperses Misfortunes.

---

[1] The Heaven of the south. 180 deg.

The Nine Heavens Sagely Mother.

The Nine Heavens Primordial Sovereign of Supreme Unity.

The Nine Heavens Great Spirit Who Oversees Life.

The Northern Dipper Sovereign of the Seven Primordial Stars.

The Southern Dipper Sovereign of the Six Superintendent Stars.

The Dipper Sovereign of The Stars that Establish Life on the Auspicious Constellation of one's Fundamental Destiny.

Each of these were followed by an entourage of ministers clerics and numinous officials, and Golden Youths and Jade Maidens and a sagely assembly beyond count.

At that moment, all were joined in congregation.

They Kowtowed in reverent worship and made offerings of incense while flowers were strewn about.

Pacing the void in loops and whorls, they came to kneel before the Dao[2], listening attentively to these words on the Doctrines[3].

---

[2] Taishang Laojun, the deified/personified Dao.

[3] Also methods.

Taishang Laojun extensively proclaimed the essentials and mysteries, declaring these instructions to the Five Directions, the Five Elders, and each of the assembled Sages, saying:

In the deep past, I was within Hundun[4]. Heaven and Earth had yet to be divided and the origin and transformations were as yet one substance.

Then the Qi spread in all ten directions, resulting in the formation of the ten thousand manifestations.

Heaven was generated. Earth was generated.

Yin carried, while Yang encircled.

Yang Qi ascended upward, transforming and generating the layered heavens.[5]

Yin Qi descended downward, transforming and generating the layered earths.[6]

The remaining Qi of Yang transformed into the male.

The remaining Qi of Yin transformed into the female.

These two Qi of Yin and Yang mixed together, naturally.

Birth after birth, death after death, endlessly.

---

[4] The primordial chaos at the beginning of time/space.

[5] Celestial layers.

[6] Terrestrial layers including the Hells.

Thus is the existence of humanity.

And so it is with humanity that there is Karma and its causes.

There is good and there is evil.

There is long and there is short[7].

There is the noble and there is the humble.

There is wealth and there is poverty.

Good and evil are recompensed as a shadow accompanies a form, like the echo responds to the voice.

Doing good has good results.

Doing evil has evil results.

Sowing orchid seeds results in fragrance.

Sowing millet results in grain.

Doing good results in blessings descending.

Doing evil results in disaster descending.

Every one of these is the defined relationship of cause and effect.

Each of them show what results follow, as blessings or repercussions.[8]

---

[7] Lifespan.

[8] These are the laws of Karma.

Even though those of mankind are born down in the world, their destiny relates to the heavens aloft.

As for the life of mankind, they have the crown of their heads in the sky the soles of their feet on the earth, they maintain both Yin and Yang.

Each one maintains the Upright Qi of the Fives Phases, each one is provided for by the Five Dippers.

The Auspicious Constellation of their Fundamental Destiny[9] corresponds to the twelve astrological signs.

So too:[10]

Those born under the Jia and Yi Stems are governed by the Eastern Dipper.

Those born under the Bing and Ding Stems are governed by the Southern Dipper.

Those born under the Wu and Ji Stems are governed by the Central Dipper.

Those born under the Geng and Xin Stems are governed by the Western Dipper.

Those born under the Ren and Gui Stems are governed by the Northern Dipper.[11]

---

[9] Birthdate.

[10] The twelve signs correspond to the Earthly Branches. Here, in addition to the twelve, the ten Celestial Stems are also taken into account. Numerically, the ten in pairs fit with the five dippers without remainders.

[11] These correspondences follow the phase correspondence of the Celestial Stems.

At the moment when life is concentrated[12], each one is endowed with the True Qi of the

Five Phases.

These True Qi swirl and combine.

They knot and ripen to become the fetus.

Encompassed and encircled by the Ten Directions, the pre-heaven life Qi of the Ten

Directions.

Embraced and enwrapped in the primordial beginnings.[13]

There, within the unfathomable depths of dark obscurity, is obtained the essence of life.

There, within the dim and faint blur, is obtained the substance of creation.

Look! I cannot be seen. Listen! I cannot be heard.

Abandon all extremes. This is the subtle Dao.

The subtle Dao is within all mankind.

Do not be frivolously remiss and lose it!

To be remiss and lose it is exceedingly easy.

To conserve and protect it is exceedingly difficult.

Many are perplexed concerning the True Dao.

They chase after heretical sources.

---

[12] Conception.

[13] That which is embraced and enwrapped is the developing human form.

Many find pleasure in licentiousness and killing.

Many find pleasure in craving and violence.[14]

Thus many sink into the earthly prisons.[15]

These multitudes then lose their Human form.[16]

At the moment when life is received:

The Five Dipper Star Sovereigns,

the multitudes of the Nine Heavens sages,

those who govern life and good fortune,

those who govern wealth and poverty,

those who govern length and brevity,[17]

those who govern the auspicious and the inauspicious,

all will cause every living being to receive the effects of their own causes.[18]

If, within the days spent in this realm,[19] a person reveres the Great Dao,

---

[14] These are ways that are inconsistent with the Daoist Precepts.

[15] Hells.

[16] Leave the path of human rebirth.

[17] Of life-span.

[18] This list enumerates the arbiters of karmic results, which all sentient beings are subject to.

[19] This lifetime.

makes offerings to the Celestial Worthies,

provides filial support to one's father and mother,

is in mutual harmony with all six relations[20],

is not jealous or envious,

is not craving or licentious.

Who perseveres in maintaining abstentions and precepts.

Who does good deeds and makes supportive offerings.[21]

Who keeps the Three Precepts, the Five Precepts, the Ten Precepts, the Twelve Precepts Permitting Alliance, or the Fourteen Precepts for Restraining the Body.

Who maintains the Twenty-four Precepts, the Thirty-six Precepts, the Seventy-two precepts, the One-hundred-and-Eight Precepts, or the Three-hundred Great Precepts.

Who cultivate the Shangqing Abstentions, the Abstentions of the Golden Register, the Abstentions of the Three Origins, the Abstentions of the Three and Seven.

Who maintains the Abstentions of the days of Gengshen, Jiazi[22], and one's Fundamental Destiny.

---

[20] The six traditional or Confucian relations: father, mother, elder sibling, younger sibling, spouse and children.

[21] This term 緣 can mean causes for karma, but also, temple offerings.

[22] Gengshen and Jiazi stem-branch combination are common days for a variety of practices, here it is specifically fasting.

If these Abstentions and Precepts are maintained, and there be a good man or good woman, they will, upon the day of their reception and maintenance of these Abstentions and Precepts have their names connected to the celestials.

In their migration through the realms,[23] in every birth, they will not lose their human form.

They will have wealth and rank and be intelligent and bright.

Among the rest of mankind, they will be remarkable and outstanding.

Their five physical constituents[24] will be complete and ample.

Their Ten Distinctions[25] will be especially impressive.

Now, in all cases of human life, the True Qi is conferred upon each from the Five Elder Imperial Sovereigns of the Five Directions.

This, along with the Golden Petition Numinous Talismans, naturally swirl and combine.

This transformation and generation becomes the living human.

I now proclaim and expound:[26]

---

[23] Six realms of cyclic rebirth.

[24] Tendons, Vessels, Muscles, Hair and Skin, and Bones. All of which are Five Phase correspondent, which is consequential in this context of the the five talismans.

[25] Marks or indications in form, that indicate one's karma. These are the traits used in physiognomy and fortune telling.

[26] This is still Taishang Laojun speaking. What follows are the five seals/talismans of the five dippers, and the incantations that activate them.

The First True Writ and Divine Incantation of the Eastern Golden Seal Numinous Talisman.

Nine Qi of the east.

Initiated in the Azure Heavens.

The Initiating Elder of the Azure Numina.

The Celestial Sovereign of the Nine Qi.

The perfected person who presses down the brush.

Downward, governing the bodies of mankind.

The virtue of wood, knotting and ripening.

Gathering in the Dao, uniting the perfected.

This seal, this numinous talisman, protects the liver within the human.

If this person's liver becomes diseased, write this in cinnabar ink,[27] reduce it to ashes and give to the person.

They will be cured immediately.[28]

---

[27] This is a direct translation. We do not suggest using cinnabar ink.

[28] Chinese language incantation and talisman on the following two pages.

東 方 第 一 金 章 靈 符 真 文
Dōng fāng dì yī jīn zhāng líng fú zhēn wén

神 咒：
shén zhòu:

東 方 九 炁， 始 青 天 中。
Dōng fāng jiǔ qì, shǐ qīng tiān zhōng.
青 靈 始 老， 九 炁 天 君。
Qīng líng shǐ lǎo, jiǔ qì tiān jūn.
真 人 按 筆， 下 注 人 身。
Zhēn rén àn bǐ, xià zhù rén shēn.
木 德 結 秀， 會 道 合 真。
Mù dé jié xiù, huì dào hé zhēn.

14

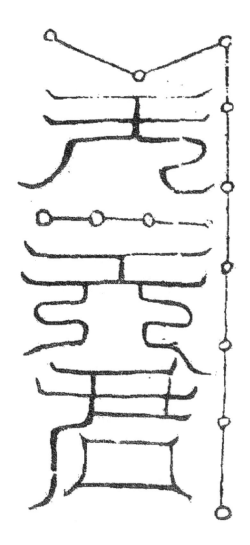

The Second True Writ and Divine Incantation of the Southern Golden Seal Numinous Talisman.

Three Qi of the south.

Red Numina Cinnabar Heaven.

The Perfected Elder of the Cinnabar Numina.

The Celestial Sovereign of the Three Qi.

The Overseer of Destiny, the Overseer of the Records.

The Spirit Worthy of the Scarlet Tower.

The virtue of fire, brightening and ripening.

Gathering in the Dao, uniting the perfected.

This seal, this numinous talisman, protects the heart within the human.

If this person's heart becomes diseased, write this in cinnabar ink, reduce it to ashes and give to the person.

They will be cured immediately.[29]

---

[29] Chinese language incantation and talisman on the following two pages.

南 方 第 二 金 章 靈 符 真 文
Nán fāng dì èr jīn zhāng líng fú zhēn wén

神 咒：
shén zhòu:

南 方 三 氣， 赤 靈 丹 天。
Nán fāng sān qì, chì líng dān tiān.
丹 靈 真 老， 三 氣 天 君。
Dān líng zhēn lǎo, sān qì tiān jūn.
司 命 司 錄， 絳 闕 尊 神。
Sī mìng sī lù, jiàng què zūn shén.
火 德 明 秀， 會 道 合 真。
Huǒ dé míng xiù, huì dào hé zhēn.

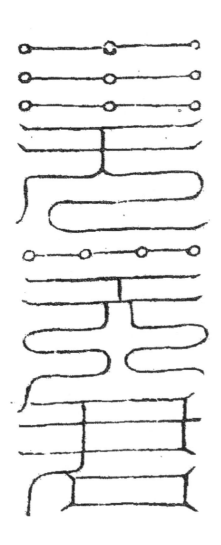

The Third True Writ and Divine Incantation of the Central Golden Seal

Numinous Talisman.

The Chief Inspector of the Numinous multitude.

The Twelfth Heaven.

The Original Numina and Original Elder.

The Celestial Sovereign of the Twelfth.

Keeper of all registers and collated records.

Governor and guardian of the Spleen Spirit.

The virtue of soil, guarding and ripening.

Gathering in the Dao, uniting the perfected.

This seal, this numinous talisman, protects the spleen within the human.

If this person's spleen becomes diseased, write this in cinnabar ink, reduce it to ashes and give to the person.

They will be cured immediately.[30]

---

[30] Chinese language incantation and talisman on the following two pages.

中　央　第　三　金　章　靈　符　真　文
Zhōng yāng dì sān jīn zhāng líng fú zhēn wén

神　咒：
shén zhòu:

總　監　眾　靈，　十　二　之　天。
Zǒng jiān zhòng líng, shí èr zhī tiān.
元　靈　元　老，　十　二　天　君。
Yuán líng yuán lǎo, shi èr tiān jūn.
都　錄　校　籍，　主　鎮　脾　神。
Dōu lù xiào jí, zhǔ zhèn pí shén.
土　德　鎮　秀，　會　道　合　真。
Tǔ dé zhèn xiù, huì dào hé zhēn.

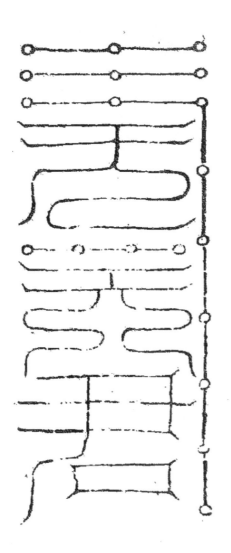

The Fourth True Writ and Divine Incantation of the Western Golden Seal Numinous Talisman.

The Seven Qi of the west.

The Heaven of Supreme White.[31]

The White Numina Imperial Elder.

The Celestial Sovereign of the Seven Qi.

The registrar of names and pacifier of Po.

Governor and guardian of the Lung Spirit.

The virtue of metal, hardening and ripening.

Gathering in the Dao, uniting the perfected.

This seal, this numinous talisman, protects the lungs within the human.

If this person's lungs become diseased, write this in cinnabar ink, reduce it to ashes and give to the person.

They will be cured immediately.[32]

---

[31] Taibai 太白 is also the name for Venus, the planet with five phase correspondence to metal.

[32] Chinese language incantation and talisman on the following two pages.

西 方 第 四 金 章 靈 符 真 文
Xī fāng dì sì jīn zhāng líng fú zhēn wén

神 咒：
shén zhòu:

西 方 七 氣， 太 白 之 天。
Xī fāng qī qì, tài bái zhī tiān.
皓 靈 皇 老， 七 氣 天 君。
Hào líng huáng lǎo, qī qì tiān jūn.
記 名 安 魄， 主 鎮 肺 神。
Jì míng ān pò, zhǔ zhèn fèi shén.
金 德 堅 秀， 會 道 合 真。
Jīn dé jiān xiù, huì dào hé zhēn.

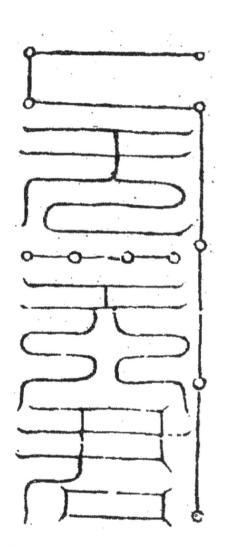

The Fifth True Writ and Divine Incantation of the Northern Golden Seal Numinous Talisman.

The Five Qi of the north.

The Heaven of the Obscure Center.

The Five Numina and Obscure Elder.

The Celestial Sovereign of the Five Qi.

Pursuer of life, scatterer of death.

Governor and guardian of the Kidney Spirit.

The virtue of water, benefitting and ripening.

Gathering in the Dao, uniting the perfected.

This seal, this numinous talisman, protects the kidneys within the human.

If this person's kidneys become diseased, write this in cinnabar ink, reduce it to ashes and give to the person.

They will be cured immediately.[33]

---

[33] Chinese language incantation and talisman on the following two pages.

北 方 第 五 金 章 靈 符 真 文
Běi fāng dì wǔ jīn zhāng líng fú zhēn wén

神 咒：
shén zhòu:

北 方 五 氣， 玄 中 之 天。
Běi fāng wǔ qì, xuán zhōng zhī tiān.

五 靈 玄 老， 五 氣 天 君。
Wǔ líng xuán lǎo, wǔ qì tiān jūn.

追 生 落 死， 主 鎮 腎 神。
Zhuī shēng luò sǐ, zhǔ zhèn shèn shén.

水 德 善 秀， 會 道 合 真。
Shuǐ dé shàn xiù, huì dào hé zhēn.

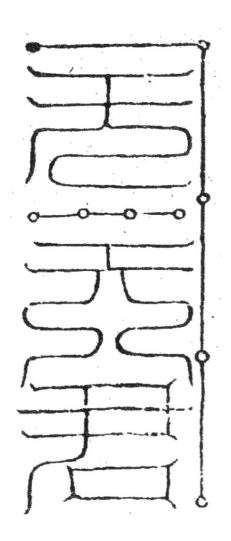

31

At that time, Laojun, again expounded upon these True writs and Divine Incantations of the Five Directions.

These numinous talismans, True Writs and Divine Incantations beckon to the Star Sovereigns of the Five Directions and Five Dippers.

Each employ the Five Dipper Star Sovereigns, utilizing the Golden Writings and Jade Seals, each one relies upon their associated direction.

They are bound to receive and maintain, to infuse life into the realm of mankind.

By these means, these Numinous Talismans and writs calm and defend the five organs, each one defending the human body.

The innate nature and destiny of the common person results and follows the life giving Qi of the Nine Heavens,

the Five Dipper Star Sovereigns, and the numinous spirits in charge of the Auspicious Constellation of their Fundamental Destiny.

If however, there is a person who not only has the capacity to understand their own root and tendril[34], but also engages in the three days of the Three Origins,[35] the Five

---

[34] Be aware of the nature of cause and effect concerning Karma and its ramifications on life circumstances.

[35] See Sanguan jing for these dates and practices.

Sacrifices,[36] one's day of birth and Fundamental Destiny, and the descending days of the Northern Dipper.[37]

If they then set up and arrange an altar, and rigorously follow the memorials and libations and make offerings to the Five Elders of the Five Directions who have given you incarnate life.

For this multitude of sages who have concentrated life;

the Five Dipper Star Sovereigns,

and the Auspicious Constellation of Ones Fundamental Destiny, one should make offerings and dedications of wealth.

Be reciprocal with those sagely multitudes who have infused your body with life, and caused you to be born within China,[38]

allowed you to encounter the Great Dao, and have sheltered and protected you with kindness.

At the moment of birth the celestial administration and the terrestrial headquarters pledge and bestow the wealth of ones fundamental destiny.

---

[36] These are five sacrifice days throughout the calendar year.

[37] See the Beidou jing for these dates and practices.

[38] A stable country where the Dao is taught and can be heard.

Those born under the Jia and Yi Stems belong to the Nine Qi of the Eastern Dipper. At the time that these people receive life, they are endowed with ninety-thousand strings of silver coins.

Those born under the Bing and Ding Stems belong to the Three Qi of the Southern Dipper. At the time that these people receive life, they are endowed with thirty-thousand strings of silver coins.

Those born under the Wu and Ji Stems belong to the Twelve Qi of the Central Dipper. At the time that these people receive life, they are endowed with one-hundred-and-twenty-thousand strings of silver coins.

Those born under the Geng and Xin Stems belong to the Seven Qi of the Western Dipper. At the time that these people receive life, they are endowed with ninety-thousand strings of silver coins.

Those born under the Ren and Gui Stems belong to Five Qi of the Norther Dipper.

At the time that these people receive life, they are endowed with fifty-thousand strings of silver coins.

If there be a good and faithful man or woman, who propagates their endowment for doing good, and never severs their endowment for doing good.

Then they will, for incarnation after incarnation continue to be born as a human.

It is imperative that they make libations and presentations of their fundamental destiny account to the Five Dippers.

The Celestial Administration and the Terrestrial Headquarters each have these laws proclaimed in writing.

For the twelve fundamental destinies[39] there are twelve Spirits of the Treasuries.

For those born under the Zi branch, they are within the first treasury.

For those born under the Chen branch, they are within the second treasury.

For those born under the Shen branch, they are within the third treasury.

For those born under the Hai branch, they are within the forth treasury.

For those born under the Mao branch, they are within the fifth treasury.

For those born under the Wei branch, they are within the sixth treasury.

---

[39] The Earthly Branches and their date associations with ones birth.

For those born under the Yin branch, they are within the seventh treasury.

For those born under the Wu branch, they are within the eighth treasury.

For those born under the Xu branch, they are within the ninth treasury.

For those born under the Is branch, they are within the tenth treasury.

For those born under the You branch, they are within the eleventh treasury.

For those born under the Chou branch, they are within the twelfth treasury.

So it is, that when people are born they have a destined storehouse of wealth and good fortune.

If a person, on the day of their fundamental destiny, makes sufficient burnt offerings and libations without scarcity or deficiency, then they will soon encounter peace and happiness.

Their travels will be open and unobstructed.

Their auspiciousness will be entirely favorable.

Their wishes will all be satisfied.

Their fundamental destiny star official will bequeath upon them, shelter and protection.

Their lifespan will be sustained.

When they die they will not lose their human form.

They will attain rebirth with high rank and wealth.

They will be presided over by both the military and civil stars,

and the stars of wealth and good fortune.

The Five happinesses[40] will shine and scintillate upon their bodily life and fetal palace.

They will have peace, happiness and a long life.

They will not encounter conditions that tempt them to do evil.

Should there be a man or woman born into impoverished conditions, who lack the means

to set forth memorials and libations.

They can, upon the day of their fundamental destiny, reverently request a Daoist priest to

recite these Treasured Scriptures of the Golden Seals of the Five Dippers, once, twice,

three times, or even five times.

Either in a temple or in the home.

Or they can steadfastly recite it themselves.

Every recitation removes a debt[41] of ten-thousand strings of cash.

Additionally they can steadfastly recite, with total devotion;

"Tuohua shousheng Tianzun"[42]

---

[40] Longevity, wealth, health, love of virtue, and a natural death.

[41] As shown above, each individual is indebted to the immortals a certain amount of celestial cash.

[42] A mantra to the deities to whom we entrust our leaving one form and being born into the next, ie. the deities enumerated in this scripture.

This can be repeated one-thousand or ten-thousand times.

Thus, when future lives are again entrusted within mankind, there will be three incarnations into a male body.

Their five physical constituents will be complete and ample.

Their Ten Distinctions will be especially impressive.

If they are in every way, respectful and reverent, they will obtain and encounter the unsurpassed upright and true Dao.

Just then,

The Five Elder Imperial Sovereigns of the Five Directions,

The Star Sovereigns of the Five Dippers,

The Southern Dipper Sovereign of the Six Superintendent Stars.

The Northern Dipper Sovereign of the Seven Primordial Stars.

The Nine Heavens Sagely Multitude,

The Star Sovereign of one's Fundamental Destiny,

The Star Sovereign of the Primordial Constellation,

ministers, clerics and numinous officials,

Golden Youths and Jade maidens,

all of these Spirit Immortals had congregated.

Having heard Laojun expound this perfected scripture they were all at once joyful and delighted.

They formally expressed their thanks to the primordial origin.

Each one vowed to accept and maintain faith.

Then,

The Imperial Sovereign Initial Elder came forth from within the assembled and kneeled.

He then composed this verse, formally expressed his thanks, politely took his leave and departed.

Kowtow before the Highest Worthy of the Perfect Origin.

With single minded faith beyond comprehension.

Profound doctrine such as this has never before been known.

On this day and this hour it is entirely obtained.

It can open the light, brilliantly, where the was darkness.

Those good doctors use these to cure diseases and maladies.

These excellent and wonderful divine incantations of the Five Numinous Talismans.

Each of you, vow to take refuge and maintain faith!

The Perfected Scripture of the Life Receiving Golden Seals of the Five Dippers as Spoken by Taishang Laojun

CHINESE TEXT WITH PINYIN
THE PERFECTED SCRIPTURE OF THE LIFE
RECEIVING GOLDEN SEALS OF THE FIVE
DIPPERS AS SPOKEN BY TAISHANG LAOJUN

太 上 老 君 說
tài shàng lǎo jūn shuō

五 斗 金 章 受 生 真 經
wǔ dòu jīn zhāng shòu shēng zhēn jīng

爾 時，
ěr shí,

太 上 老 君 在 太 清 境 上、
tài shàng lǎo jūn zài tài qīng jìng shàng,

大 赤 天 中、黃 金 殿 內，
dà chì tiān zhōng, huáng jīn diàn nèi,

召 五 老 帝 君 及 東 斗 注 筭
zhào wǔ lǎo dì jūn jí dōng dòu zhù suàn

君、南 斗 上 生 君、西 斗 記 名
jūn, nán dòu shàng shēng jūn, xī dòu jì míng

君、
jūn,

北 斗 落 死 君、中 斗 總 監 君、
Běi dòu luò sǐ jūn, zhōng dòu zǒng jiān jūn,

九 天 生 神 君、九 天 注 生 君、
jiǔ tiān shēng shén jūn, jiǔ tiān zhù shēng jūn,

九 天 注 祿 君、
jiǔ tiān zhù lù jūn,

九 天 掌 籍 掌 算 君、
jiǔ tiān zhǎng jí zhǎng suàn jūn,

九 天 財 庫 祿 庫 君、
jiǔ tiān cái kù lù kù jūn,

九天消災散禍君、
jiǔ tiān xiāo zāi sàn huò jūn,

九天聖母九天太一元君、
jiǔ tiān shèng mǔ jiǔ tiān tài yī yuán jūn,

九天監生大神、
jiǔ tiān jiān shēng dà shén,

北斗七元星君、
Běi dòu qī yuán xīng jūn,

南斗六司星君、
nán dòu liù sī xīng jūn,

本命元辰建生星斗君，
běn mìng yuán chén jiàn shēng xīng dòu jūn,

各隨本部功曹靈官、
gè suí běn bù gōng cáo líng guān,

金童玉女無量聖眾，
jīn tóng yù nǚ wú liàng shèng zhòng,

一時同會，稽首禮拜，
yī shí tóng huì, jī shǒu lǐ bài,

燒香散花，步虛旋繞，
shāo xiāng sàn huā, bù xū xuán rào,

長跪道前，諦聽法言。
zhǎng guì dào qián, dì tīng fǎ yán.

太上老君廣宣要妙，
Tài shàng lǎo jūn guǎng xuān yào miào,

告示五方五老一切
gào shì wǔ fāng wǔ lǎo yī qiè

聖　眾　曰：
Shèng　zhòng　yuē:

吾　昔　於　混　沌　之　中，
Wú　xī　yú　hùn　dùn　zhī　zhōng,

天　地　未　分，元　化　體　一，
tiān　de　wèi　fēn,　yuán　huà　tǐ　yī,

布　氣　十　方，
bù　qì　shí　fāng,

成　就　萬　象，生　天　生　地，
chéng　jiù　wàn　xiàng,　shēng　tiān　shēng　di,

負　陰　抱　陽，陽　氣　上　升，
fù　yīn　bào　yáng,　yáng　qì　shàng　shēng,

化　生　諸　天，陰　氣　下　降，
huà　shēng　zhū　tiān,　yīn　qì　xià　jiàng,

化　生　諸　地，
huà　shēng　zhū　di,

陽　之　餘　氣　化　為　男　子，
Yáng　zhī　yú　qì　huà　wèi　nán　zǐ,

陰　之　餘　氣　化　為　女　人，
yīn　zhī　yú　qì　huà　wèi　nǚ　rén,

陰　陽　二　氣，混　合　自　然，
yīn　yáng　èr　qì,　hùn　hé　zì　rán,

生　生　化　化，乃　有　人　倫。
shēng　shēng　huà　huà,　nǎi　yǒu　rén　lún.

既　有　人　倫，宿　命　因　緣，
Jì　yǒu　rén　lún,　sù　mìng　yīn　yuán,

有善有惡，有長有短，
yǒu shàn yǒu è, yǒu zhǎng yǒu duǎn,
有貴有賤，有富有貧，
yǒu guì yǒu jiàn, yǒu fù yǒu pín,
善惡之報，如影逐形，
shàn è zhī bào, rú yǐng zhú xíng,
如響應聲，作善善應，
rú xiǎng yīng shēng, zuò shàn shàn yīng,
作惡惡成，種蘭得香，
Zuò è è chéng, zhǒng lán dé xiāng,
種粟得糧，為善降祥，
zhǒng sù dé liáng, wèi shàn jiàng xiáng,
為惡降殃，一切因緣，
wèi è jiàng yāng, yī qiè yīn yuán,
皆由福業。
jiē yóu fú yè.
且人生下土，命係上天，
Qiě rén shēng xià tǔ, mìng xì shàng tiān,
人之生也，頂天履地，
rén zhī shēng yě, dǐng tiān lǚ di,
有陰有陽，各有五行正氣，
yǒu yīn yǒu yáng, gè yǒu wǔ xíng zhèng qì,
各有五斗所管，本命元辰，
gè yǒu wǔ dòu suǒ guǎn, běn mìng yuán chén,
十二相屬，
shí èr xiāng shǔ,

且甲乙生人東斗注生，
Qiě jiǎ yǐ shēng rén dōng dòu zhù shēng,

丙丁生人南斗注生，
bǐng dīng shēng rén nán dòu zhù shēng,

戊己生人中斗注生，
wù jǐ shēng rén zhōng dòu zhù shēng,

庚辛生人西斗注生，
gēng xīn shēng rén xī dòu zhù shēng,

壬癸生人北斗注生，
én guǐ shēng rén běi dòu zhù shēng,

注生之時，各稟五行真氣，
zhù shēng zhī shí, gè bǐng wǔ xíng zhēn qì,

真氣混合，結秀成胎，
zhēn qì hùn hé, jié xiù chéng tāi,

受胎十月，周回十方，
shòu tāi shí yuè, zhōu huí shí fāng,

十方生氣。
shí fāng shēng qì.

包羅元始，杳杳冥冥，
Bāo luó yuán shǐ, yǎo yǎo míng míng,

其中有精，恍恍惚惚，
qí zhōng yǒu jīng, huǎng huǎng hū hū,

其中有物，視不見我，
qí zhōng yǒu wù, shì bù jiàn wǒ,

聽不得聞，離種種邊，
tīng bù dé wén, lí zhǒng zhǒng biān,

名為妙道。妙道在人，
不可輕失，失之甚易，
保之甚難，多迷真道，
多逐邪源，多好淫殺，
多好貪嗔，多沉地獄，
多失人身。受生之時，
五斗星君，九天聖眾，
注生注祿，注富注貧，
注長注短，注吉注凶，
皆由眾生，自作自受。
若人在世之日，心崇大道，
供養天尊，孝順父母，
和同六親，不嫉不妒，

不貪不婬，或持齋戒，
bù tān bù yín, huò chí zhāi jiè,
或作善緣，或受三戒五戒，
huò zuò shàn yuán, huò shòu sān jiè wǔ jiè,
十戒十二可從戒，
shí jiè shí èr kě cóng jiè,
十四持身戒，二十四戒，
shí sì chí shēn jiè, èr shí sì jiè,
三十六戒，
sān shí liù jiè,
七十二戒，一百八戒，
qī shí èr jiè, yī bǎi bā jiè,
三百大戒；或修上清齋、
sān bǎi dà jiè; huò xiū shàng qīng zhāi,
金籙齋、三元齋、三七齋、
jīn lù zhāi, sān yuán zhāi, sān qī zhāi,
庚申齋、甲子齋、本命齋，
gēng shēn zhāi, jiǎ zi zhāi, běn mìng zhāi,
如是齋戒，
rú shì zhāi jiè,
若有善男子善女人受持
ruò yǒu shàn nán zi shàn nǚ rén shòu chí
之者，名係天人，世世生生，
zhī zhě, míng xì tiān rén, shì shì shēng shēng,
不失人身，富貴聰明，
bù shī rén shēn, fù guì cōng míng,

人中殊勝，五體具足，
rén zhōng shū shèng, wǔ tǐ jù zú,
十相端嚴。且人之生也，
shí xiāng duān yán. Qiě rén zhī shēng yě,
皆受五方五老帝君各降
jiē shòu wǔ fāng wǔ lǎo dì jūn gè jiàng
真氣，金章靈符，混合自然，
zhēn qì, jīn zhāng líng fú, hùn hé zì rán,
化生為人。
huà shēng wèi rén.

吾今宣說：
Wú jīn xuān shuō:

東方第一金章靈符真文
Dōng fāng dì yī jīn zhāng líng fú zhēn wén

神咒：
shén zhòu:

東方九炁，始青天中。
Dōng fāng jiǔ qì, shǐ qīng tiān zhōng.
青靈始老，九炁天君。
Qīng líng shǐ lǎo, jiǔ qì tiān jūn.
真人按筆，下注人身。
Zhēn rén àn bǐ, xià zhù rén shēn.
木德結秀，會道合真。
Mù dé jié xiù, huì dào hé zhēn.

49

此 章 靈 符 鎮 人 肝 中，
Cǐ zhāng líng fú zhèn rén gān zhōng,
若 人 肝 受 病，
ruò rén gān shòu bìng,
以 朱 書 燒 灰 服 之， 立 愈。
yǐ zhū shū shāo huī fú zhī, lì yù.

南 方 第 二 金 章 靈 符 真 文
Nán fāng dì èr jīn zhāng líng fú zhēn wén

神 咒：
shén zhòu:
南 方 三 氣， 赤 靈 丹 天。
Nán fāng sān qì, chì líng dān tiān.
丹 靈 真 老， 三 氣 天 君。
Dān líng zhēn lǎo, sān qì tiān jūn.
司 命 司 錄， 絳 闕 尊 神。
Sī mìng sī lù, jiàng què zūn shén.
火 德 明 秀， 會 道 合 真。
Huǒ dé míng xiù, huì dào hé zhēn.
此 章 靈 符 鎮 人 心 中，
Cǐ zhāng líng fú zhèn rén xīn zhōng,
若 人 心 受 病，
ruò rén xīn shòu bìng,
以 朱 書 燒 灰 服 之， 立 愈。
yǐ zhū shū shāo huī fú zhī, lì yù.

中央第三金章靈符真文
Zhōng yāng dì sān jīn zhāng líng fú zhēn wén

神咒：
shén zhòu:

總監眾靈，十二之天。
Zǒng jiān zhòng líng, shí èr zhī tiān.

元靈元老，十二天君。
Yuán líng yuán lǎo, shi èr tiān jūn.

都錄校籍，主鎮脾神。
Dōu lù xiào jí, zhǔ zhèn pí shén.

土德鎮秀，會道合真。
Tǔ dé zhèn xiù, huì dào hé zhēn.

此章靈符鎮人脾中，
Cǐ zhāng líng fú zhèn rén pí zhōng,

若人脾受病，
ruò rén pí shòu bìng,

以朱書燒灰服之，立愈。
yǐ zhū shū shāo huī fú zhī, lì yù

西方第四金章靈符真文
Xī fāng dì sì jīn zhāng líng fú zhēn wén

神咒：
shén zhòu:

西方七氣，太白之天。
Xī fāng qī qì, tài bái zhī tiān.

皓靈皇老，七氣天君。
Hào líng huáng lǎo, qī qì tiān jūn.

記名安魄，主鎮肺神。
Jì míng ān pò, zhǔ zhèn fèi shén.

金德堅秀，會道合真。
Jīn dé jiān xiù, huì dào hé zhēn.

此章靈符鎮人肺中，
Cǐ zhāng líng fú zhèn rén fèi zhōng,

若人肺受病，
ruò rén fèi shòu bìng,

以朱書燒灰服之，立愈。
yǐ zhū shū shāo huī fú zhī, lì yù.

北方第五金章靈符真文
Běi fāng dì wǔ jīn zhāng líng fú zhēn wén

神咒：
shén zhòu:

北方五氣，玄中之天。
Běi fāng wǔ qì, xuán zhōng zhī tiān.

五靈玄老，五氣天君。
Wǔ líng xuán lǎo, wǔ qì tiān jūn.

追生落死，主鎮腎神。
Zhuī shēng luò sǐ, zhǔ zhèn shèn shén.

水德善秀，會道合真。
Shuǐ dé shàn xiù, huì dào hé zhēn.

52

此 章 靈 符 鎮 人 腎 中，
Cǐ zhāng líng fú zhèn rén shèn zhōng,

若 人 腎 受 病，
ruò rén shèn shòu bìng,

以 朱 書 燒 灰 服 之， 立 愈。
yǐ zhū shū shāo huī fú zhī, lì yù

爾 時，
er shi

老 君 再 說 此 五 方 真 文 神
Lǎo jūn zài shuō cǐ wǔ fāng zhēn wén shén

咒， 即 召 五 方 五 斗 星 君，
zhòu, jí zhào wǔ fāng wǔ dòu xīng jūn,

降 此 靈 符 真 文 神 咒，
jiàng cǐ líng fú zhēn wén shén zhòu,

各 授 五 斗 星 君，
gè shòu wǔ dòu xīng jūn,

即 以 金 書 玉 篆， 各 依 其 方，
jí yǐ jīn shū yù zhuàn, gè yī qí fāng,

總 得 受 持， 注 生 世 人，
zǒng dé shòu chí, zhù shēng shì rén,

以 此 靈 文 安 鎮 五 臟，
yǐ cǐ líng wén ān zhèn wǔ zàng,

各 鎮 人 身。 凡 人 性 命，
gè zhèn rén shēn. Fán rén xìng mìng,

皆 由 九 天 生 氣 五 斗 星 君
jiē yóu jiǔ tiān shēng qì wǔ dòu xīng jūn

53

本命元辰主掌靈神，
běn mìng yuán chén zhǔ zhǎng líng shén,

若復有人能知根本，
ruò fù yǒu rén néng zhī gēn běn,

但遇三元五臘本命生辰
dàn yù sān yuán wǔ là běn mìng shēng chén

北斗下日，嚴置壇場，
běi dòu xià rì, yán zhì tán chǎng,

隨力章醮，供養五方五老，
suí lì zhāng jiào, gōng yǎng wǔ fāng wǔ lǎo,

乃吾化身注生聖眾五斗
nǎi wú huà shēn zhù shēng shèng zhòng wǔ dòu

星君、本命元辰，醮獻錢財，
xīng jūn, běn mìng yuán chén, jiào xiàn qián cái,

以答眾真，注我生身，
yǐ dá zhòng zhēn, zhù wǒ shēng shēn,

得生中國，
dé shēng zhōng guó,

得遇大道廕佑之恩。
dé yù dà dào yìn yòu zhī ēn.

當生之時，
Dāng shēng zhī shí,

天曹地府願許本命錢，
tiān cáo de fǔ yuàn xǔ běn mìng qián,

且甲乙生人，
qiě jiǎ yǐ shēng rén,

命屬東斗九氣，
mìng shǔ dōng dòu jiǔ qì,
為人受生之時，
wèi rén shòu shēng zhī shí,
曾許本命銀錢九萬貫文；
céng xǔ běn mìng yín qián jiǔ wàn guàn wén;
丙丁生人，命屬南斗三氣，
bǐng dīng shēng rén, mìng shǔ nán dòu sān qì,
為人受生之時，
wèi rén shòu shēng zhī shí,
曾許本命銀錢三萬貫文；
céng xǔ běn mìng yín qián sān wàn guàn wén;
戊己生人，
wù jǐ shēng rén,
命屬中斗一十二氣，
mìng shǔ zhōng dòu yī shí èr qì,
為人受生之時，
wèi rén shòu shēng zhī shí,
曾許本命銀錢一十二萬
céng xǔ běn mìng yín qián yī shí èr wàn
貫文；
guàn wén;
庚辛生人，命屬西斗七氣，
gēng xīn shēng rén, mìng shǔ xī dòu qī qì,
為人受生之時，
wèi rén shòu shēng zhī shí,

曾（céng）許（xǔ）本（běn）命（mìng）銀（yín）錢（qián）七（qī）萬（wàn）貫（guàn）文（wén）；

壬（rén）癸（guǐ）生（shēng）人（rén），命（mìng）屬（shǔ）北（běi）斗（dòu）五（wǔ）氣（qì），

為（wèi）人（rén）受（shòu）生（shēng）之（zhī）時（shí），

曾（Céng）許（xǔ）本（běn）命（mìng）銀（yín）錢（qián）五（wǔ）萬（wàn）貫（guàn）文（wén）。

若（Ruò）有（yǒu）善（shàn）信（xìn）男（nán）女（nǚ），種（zhǒng）諸（zhū）善（shàn）根（gēn），

善（shàn）根（gēn）不（bù）斷（duàn），世（shì）世（shì）為（wèi）人（rén），

當（dāng）須（xū）醮（jiào）送（sòng）五（wǔ）本（běn）命（mìng）錢（qián），

天（tiān）曹（cáo）地（de）府（fǔ）各（gè）有（yǒu）明（míng）文（wén），

十（shí）二（èr）本（běn）命（mìng），十（shí）二（èr）庫（kù）神（shén）。

子（Zi）生（shēng）之（zhī）人（rén）第（dì）一（yī）庫（kù）中（zhōng），

辰（chén）生（shēng）之（zhī）人（rén）第（dì）二（èr）庫（kù）中（zhōng），

申（shēn）生（shēng）之（zhī）人（rén）第（dì）三（sān）庫（kù）中（zhōng），

亥（hài）生（shēng）之（zhī）人（rén）第（dì）四（sì）庫（kù）中（zhōng），

卯生之人第五庫中，
mǎo shēng zhī rén dì wǔ kù zhōng,

未生之人第六庫中，
wèi shēng zhī rén dì liù kù zhōng,

寅生之人第七庫中，
yín shēng zhī rén dì qī kù zhōng,

午生之人第八庫中，
wǔ shēng zhī rén dì bā kù zhōng,

戌生之人第九庫中，
xū shēng zhī rén dì jiǔ kù zhōng,

巳生之人第十庫中，
sì shēng zhī rén dì shí kù zhōng,

酉生之人第十一庫中，
yǒu shēng zhī rén dì shí yī kù zhōng,

丑生之人第十二庫中。
chǒu shēng zhī rén dì shí èr kù zhōng.

乃是生人各有財祿命庫，
nǎi shì shēng rén gè yǒu cái lù mìng kù,

若人本命之日，
ruò rén běn mìng zhī rì,

依此燒醮了足，別無少欠，
yī cǐ shāo jiào le zú, bié wú shǎo qiàn,

即得見世安樂，出入通達，
jí dé jiàn shì ān lè, chū rù tōng dá,

吉無不利，所願如心，
jí wú bù lì, suǒ yuàn rú xīn,

自有本命星官常垂廕佑，
zì yǒu běn mìng xīng guān cháng chuí yìn yòu,

使保天年，過世之時，
shǐ bǎo tiān nián, guò shì zhī shí,

不失人身，得生富貴文武，
bù shī rén shēn, dé shēng fù guì wén wǔ,

星臨財星祿星，
xīng lín cái xīng lù xīng,

五福照曜身命胎宮，
wǔ fú zhào yào shēn mìng tāi gōng,

安樂長壽，不值惡緣。
ān lè zhǎng shòu, bù zhí è yuán.

若有男女生身果薄，
ruò yǒu nán nǚ shēng shēn guǒ báo,

無力章醮，可於本命之日，
wú lì zhāng jiào, kě yú běn mìng zhī rì,

請正一道士，或一或二，
qǐng zhèng yī dào shì, huò yī huò èr,

或三或五，或於宮觀、
huò sān huò wǔ, huò yú gōng guān,

或就家庭，持誦
huò jiù jiā tíng, chí sòng

《五斗金章寶經》，
"wǔ dòu jīn zhāng bǎo jīng"

或以自願持諷，每誦一遍，
huò yǐ zì yuàn chí fěng, měi sòng yī biàn,

折錢一萬貫文，
zhé qián yī wàn guàn wén,

又志心持念托化受生天
yòu zhì xīn chí niàn tuō huà shòu shēng tiān

尊，或千或萬，
zūn, huò qiān huò wàn,

當來托生人中，
dāng lái tuō shēng rén zhōng,

三世長為男子之身，
sān shì zhǎng wèi nán zi zhī shēn,

五體全備，十相端嚴，
wǔ tǐ quán bèi, shí xiāng duān yán,

一切恭敬，
yī qiè gōng jìng,

得遇無上正真之道。
dé yù wú shàng zhèng zhēn zhī dào.

是時五方五老帝君、
Shì shí wǔ fāng wǔ lǎo dì jūn,

五斗星君、南斗六司星君、
Wǔ dòu xīng jūn, nán dòu liù sī xīng jūn,

北斗七元星君、九天聖眾、
běi dòu qī yuán xīng jūn, jiǔ tiān shèng zhòng,

本命星官、元辰星官、
běn mìng xīng guān, yuán chén xīng guān,

功曹靈官、金童玉女、
gōng cáo líng guān, jīn tóng yù nǚ,

一會神仙，得聞老君說此真經，一時歡喜，禮謝玄元，各願受持。時有始老帝君，出班長跪，而作是偈，稽首禮謝，珍重而退。

Yī huì shén xiān, dé wén lǎo jūn shuō cǐ zhēn jīng, yī shí huān xǐ, lǐ xiè xuán yuán, gè yuàn shòu chí. Shí yǒu shǐ lǎo dì jūn, chū bān zhǎng guì, ér zuò shì jì, jī shǒu lǐ xiè, zhēn zhòng ér tuì.

稽首真元無上尊，
Jī shǒu zhēn yuán wú shàng zūn,

一心信奉不思議。
yī xīn xìn fèng bù sī yì.

如斯妙法未曾聞，
Rú sī miào fǎ wèi céng wén,

今日今時盡得之。
jīn rì jīn shí jǐn dé zhī.

能為黑暗開光明，
Néng wèi hēi àn kāi guāng míng,

能為疾病作良醫。
néng wèi jí bìng zuò liáng yī.

妙哉神咒五靈符，
Miào zāi shén zhòu wǔ líng fú,

誓願歸依各受持。
shì yuàn guī yī gè shòu chí.

太　上　老　君　說
Tài　shàng　lǎo　jūn　shuō

五　斗　金　章　受　生　真　經
wǔ　dòu　jīn　zhāng　shòu　shēng　zhēn　jīng

太上老君說五斗金章受生經

爾時
太上老君在太清境上大赤天中黃金殿內
召五老帝君及東斗注筭君南斗上生君西
斗記名君北斗落死君中斗總監君九天生
神君九天注生君九天注祿君九天掌籍掌
筭君九天財庫祿庫君九天消災散禍君九
天聖母九天太一元君九天監生大神北斗
七元星君南斗六司注生元辰建生星
斗君各隨本部功曹靈官金童玉女無量聖
眾一時同會稽首禮拜燒香散花步虛旋繞
長跪道前諦聽法言
太上老君廣宣要妙告示五方五老一切聖
眾曰吾昔於混沌之中天地未分元化體一
布氣十方成就萬象生天生地負陰抱陽陽
氣上升化生諸天陰氣下降化生諸地陽之
餘氣化為男子陰之餘氣化為女人陰陽二
氣混合自然生生化化乃有人倫既有人倫
宿命因緣有善有惡有長有短有貴有賤有
富有貧善惡之報如影逐形如響應聲作善

土命係
善應作善惡成種蘭得香種粟得粮為善降
祥為惡降殃一切因緣皆由福業且人生下
行正氣各有五斗所管本命元辰十二相屬
且甲乙生人東斗注生丙丁生人南斗注生
戊己生人中斗注生庚辛生人西斗注生壬
癸生人北斗注生之時各稟五行真氣
真氣混合結秀成胎受胎十月周回十方十
方生氣包羅元始杳杳冥冥其中有精恍恍
惚惚其中有物視不見我聽不得聞離種種
遊名為妙道妙道在人不可輕失失之甚易
保之甚難多沉地獄多失人身受生之時五
好貪嗔多逐邪源多好婬殺多
星君九天聖眾注生注祿注富注貧注長注
短注吉注凶皆由眾生自作自受若人在世
之日心崇大道供養天尊孝順父母和同六
親不嫉不妒不貪不婬或持齋戒或作善緣
或受三戒五戒十戒十二可從戒十四持身
戒二十四戒三十六戒七十二戒一百八戒

三百大戒或修上清齋金籙齋三元齋三七
齋庚申齋甲子齋本命齋如是齋戒若有善
男子善女人受持之者名係天人世世生
不失人身富貴聰明人中殊勝五體具足十
相端嚴且人之生也皆受
然化生爲人吾今宣說
五方五老帝君各降眞氣金章靈符混合自
真人擇筆　下注人身　木德結秀
東方第一金章靈符眞文神呪
東方九炁　始青天中　青靈始老　九炁天君

此章靈符鎭人肝中若人肝受病以
朱書燒灰服之立愈
南方第二金章靈符眞文神呪
南方三炁　赤靈丹天　丹靈眞老　三氣天君
司命司錄　絳闕尊神　火德明秀　會道合眞

此章靈符鎭人心中若人心受病以
朱書燒灰服之立愈
中央第三金章靈符眞文神呪
緫監衆靈　十二之天　元靈元老　十二天君
都錄校籍　主鎭脾神　土德鎭秀　會道合眞

此章靈符鎭人脾中若人脾受病以
朱書燒灰服之立愈
西方第四金章靈符眞文神呪
西方七炁　太白之天　皓靈皇老　七氣天君
記名安魄　主鎭肺神　金德堅秀　會道合眞

此章靈符鎮人肺中若人肺受病以
朱書燒灰服之立愈
北方第五金章靈符真文神呪
北方五氣 玄中之天 五靈玄老 五氣天君
迄生落死 主鎮腎神 水德善芳 會道合真

女二
十三

此章靈符鎮人腎中若人腎受病以
朱書燒灰服之立愈
爾時
老君再說此五方真文神呪即召五方五斗
星君降此靈符真文神呪各授五斗星君即

以金書玉篆各依其方總得受持注生世人
以此靈文安鎮五臟各鎮人身凡人性命皆
由九天生氣五斗星君本命元辰主掌靈神
若復有人能知根本但遇三元五臘本命生
辰北斗下日嚴置壇場隨力章醮供養五方
五老乃吾化身注生聖眾五斗星君本命元
辰醮獻錢財以答眾真注我生身得生中國
得遇大道慇佑之恩當生之時天曹地府為
許本命錢且甲乙生人命屬東斗生人為人
受生之時曾許本命銀錢九萬貫文丙丁生
人命屬南斗二氣為人受生之時曾許本命
銀錢三萬貫文戊己生人命屬中斗十一二
氣為人受生之時曾許本命銀錢十二萬
貫文庚辛生人命屬西斗生人命屬西十七萬
時曾許本命銀錢七萬貫文壬癸生人命屬
北斗五氣為人受生之時曾許本命銀錢五
萬貫文若有善信男女種諸善根善根不斷
世世為人當須醮送五本命錢天曹地府各
有明文十二本命十二庫神
子生之人第一庫中 辰生之人第二庫中

女二
十四

申生之人第三庫中　亥生之人第四庫中
卯生之人第五庫中　未生之人第六庫中
寅生之人第七庫中　午生之人第八庫中
戌生之人第九庫中　巳生之人第十庫中
酉生之人第十一庫中　丑生之人第十二庫中

乃是生人各有財祿命庫若人本命之日於
富貴文武星臨財祿星五福照曜身命胎
垂庇佑伎保天年過世之時不失人身得生
通達吉無不利所願如心目有本命星官常
此燒醮了足別無少欠即得見世安樂出入
○
宮安樂長壽不值惡緣若有男女生身果薄
無力章醮可於本命之日請正一道士或一
或二或三或五或於宮觀或就家庭持誦五
斗金章寶經或以自願持誦每誦一遍持誦
一萬貫文又志心持念托化受生天尊或千
體金備十相端嚴一切恭敬得遇無上正真
之道是時五方五老帝君五斗星君南斗六
司星君北斗七元星君九天聖眾本命星官
元辰星官功曹靈官金童玉女一會神仙得

闓

老君說此真經一時歡喜禮謝玄元各願受
持時有始老帝君出班長跪而作是偈稽首
禮謝珍重而退
稽首真元無上尊　一心信奉不思議
如斯妙法未曾聞　今日今時盍得之
能為黑暗開光明　能為疾病作良醫
妙哉神呪五靈符　誓願隨侊各安持
○太上老君說五斗金章受生經

ABOUT

Joshua Paynter

Josh is an ordained 22nd generation Daoist Priest in the Quanzhen, Longmen tradition at the Jian Fu Gong on Qingcheng Mountain, Daoist name Li Wen 理文. He is also ordained as a 25th generation Daoist Priest in the Quanzhen, Longmen tradition at the Qingyun Daoguan, Daoist name Xin Jian 信堅.

Jack Schaefer

Jack is an ordained 22nd generation Daoist Priest in the Quanzhen, Longmen tradition at the Jian Fu Gong on Qingcheng Mountain, Daoist name Li Xuan 理玄. He is also ordained as a 25th generation Daoist Priest in the Quanzhen, Longmen tradition at the Qingyun Daoguan, Daoist name Xin Yin 信銀.

**PARTING CLOUDS
DAOIST EDUCATION**

Printed in Poland
by Amazon Fulfillment
Poland Sp. z o.o., Wrocław

32827612R00045